# SONDHEIM
## FOR CLASSICAL PLAYERS

To access companion recorded piano accompaniments online, visit:
**www.halleonard.com/mylibrary**

Enter Code
1249-3957-9725-0113

ISBN: 978-1-5400-2612-5

## RILTING MUSIC, INC.

EXCLUSIVELY DISTRIBUTED BY

Visit Hal Leonard Online at
**www.halleonard.com**

Contact Us:
**Hal Leonard**
7777 West Bluemound Road
Milwaukee, WI 53213
Email: info@halleonard.com

In Europe contact:
**Hal Leonard Europe Limited**
42 Wigmore Street
Marylebone, London, W1U 2RN
Email: info@halleonardeurope.com

In Australia contact:
**Hal Leonard Australia Pty. Ltd.**
4 Lentara Court
Cheltenham, Victoria, 3192 Australia
Email: info@halleonard.com.au

# HOW TO USE HAL LEONARD ONLINE AUDIO

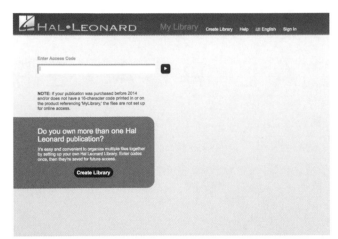

Because of the changing use of media, and the fact that fewer people are using CDs, we have made a shift to companion audio accessible online. In many cases, rather than a book with CD, we now have a book with an access code for online audio, including performances, accompaniments or diction lessons. Each copy of each book has a unique access code. We call this Hal Leonard created system "My Library." It's simple to use.

**Go to www.halleonard.com/mylibrary and enter the unique access code found on page one of a relevant book/audio package.**

The audio tracks can be streamed or downloaded. If you download the tracks on your computer, you can add the files to a CD or to your digital music library, and use them anywhere without being online. See below for comments about Apple and Android mobile devices.

There are some great benefits to the My Library system. **Playback+** is exclusive to Hal Leonard, and when connected to the Internet with this multi-functional audio player you can:

• Change tempo without changing pitch
• Transpose to any key

Optionally, you can create a My Library account, and store all the companion audio you have purchased there. Access your account online at any time, from any device, by logging into your account at www.halleonard.com/mylibrary. Technical help may be found at www.halleonard.com/mylibrary/help/

### Apple/iOS

*Question: On my iPad and iPhone, the Download links just open another browser tab and play the track. How come this doesn't really download?*

**Answer:** The Safari iOS browser will not allow you to download audio files directly in iTunes or other apps. There are several ways to work around this:

- You can download normally on your desktop computer, saving the files to iTunes. Then, you can sync your iOS device directly to your computer, or sync your iTunes content using an iCloud account.
- There are many third-party apps which allow you to download files from websites into the app's own file manager for easy retrieval and playback.

### Android

Files are always downloaded to the same location, which is a folder usually called "Downloads" (this may vary slightly depending on what browser is used (Chrome, Firefox, etc)). Chrome uses a system app called "Downloads" where files can be accessed at any time. Firefox and some other browsers store downloaded files within a "Downloads" folder in the browser itself.

Recently-downloaded files can be accessed from the Notification bar; swiping down will show the downloaded files as a new "card", which you tap on to open. Opening a file depends on what apps are installed on the Android device. Audio files are opened in the device's default audio app. If a file type does not have a default app assigned to it, the Android system alerts the user.

# CONTENTS

Pianists on the recordings: [1]Brendan Fox, [2]Ruben Piirainen, [3]Richard Walters

The price of this publication includes access to companion recorded piano accompaniments online,

for download or streaming, using the unique code found on the title page.

Visit **www.halleonard.com/mylibrary** and enter the access code.

# Anyone Can Whistle

from *Anyone Can Whistle*

Words and Music by
Stephen Sondheim

*fermatas second time only

# Agony
## from *Into the Woods*

Words and Music by
Stephen Sondheim

# The Ballad of Sweeney Todd

from *Sweeney Todd*

Words and Music by
Stephen Sondheim

**Misterioso, con moto** (♩. = 132)

# Children Will Listen

from *Into the Woods*

Words and Music by
Stephen Sondheim

# Johanna

## from *Sweeney Todd*

Words and Music by
Stephen Sondheim

# Night Waltz

from *A Little Night Music*

Words and Music by
Stephen Sondheim

# SONDHEIM
## FOR CLASSICAL PLAYERS

*Stephen Sondheim*

To access companion recorded piano accompaniments online, visit:
**www.halleonard.com/mylibrary**

Enter Code
8087-9694-8485-8618

ISBN: 978-1-5400-2612-5

## RILTING MUSIC, INC.
EXCLUSIVELY DISTRIBUTED BY
**Hal•Leonard**®

Visit Hal Leonard Online at
**www.halleonard.com**

Contact us:
**Hal Leonard**
7777 West Bluemound Road
Milwaukee, WI 53213
Email: info@halleonard.com

In Europe, contact:
**Hal Leonard Europe Limited**
42 Wigmore Street
Marylebone, London, W1U 2RN
Email: info@halleonardeurope.com

In Australia, contact:
**Hal Leonard Australia Pty. Ltd.**
4 Lentara Court
Cheltenham, Victoria, 3192 Australia
Email: info@halleonard.com.au

# HOW TO USE HAL LEONARD ONLINE AUDIO

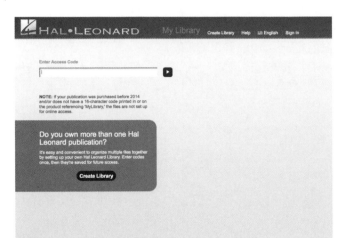

Because of the changing use of media, and the fact that fewer people are using CDs, we have made a shift to companion audio accessible online. In many cases, rather than a book with CD, we now have a book with an access code for online audio, including performances, accompaniments or diction lessons. Each copy of each book has a unique access code. We call this Hal Leonard created system "My Library." It's simple to use.

**Go to www.halleonard.com/mylibrary and enter the unique access code found on page one of a relevant book/audio package.**

The audio tracks can be streamed or downloaded. If you download the tracks on your computer, you can add the files to a CD or to your digital music library, and use them anywhere without being online. See below for comments about Apple and Android mobile devices.

There are some great benefits to the My Library system. *Playback+* is exclusive to Hal Leonard, and when connected to the Internet with this multi-functional audio player you can:

• Change tempo without changing pitch
• Transpose to any key

Optionally, you can create a My Library account, and store all the companion audio you have purchased there. Access your account online at any time, from any device, by logging into your account at www.halleonard.com/mylibrary. Technical help may be found at www.halleonard.com/mylibrary/help/

### Apple/iOS

*Question:* On my iPad and iPhone, the Download links just open another browser tab and play the track. How come this doesn't really download?

**Answer:** The Safari iOS browser will not allow you to download audio files directly in iTunes or other apps. There are several ways to work around this:

• You can download normally on your desktop computer, saving the files to iTunes. Then, you can sync your iOS device directly to your computer, or sync your iTunes content using an iCloud account.

• There are many third-party apps which allow you to download files from websites into the app's own file manager for easy retrieval and playback.

### Android

Files are always downloaded to the same location, which is a folder usually called "Downloads" (this may vary slightly depending on what browser is used (Chrome, Firefox, etc)). Chrome uses a system app called "Downloads" where files can be accessed at any time. Firefox and some other browsers store downloaded files within a "Downloads" folder in the browser itself.

Recently-downloaded files can be accessed from the Notification bar; swiping down will show the downloaded files as a new "card", which you tap on to open. Opening a file depends on what apps are installed on the Android device. Audio files are opened in the device's default audio app. If a file type does not have a default app assigned to it, the Android system alerts the user.

# CONTENTS

Pianists on the recordings: [1]Brendan Fox, [2]Ruben Piirainen, [3]Richard Walters

The price of this publication includes access to companion recorded piano accompaniments online,

for download or streaming, using the unique code found on the title page.

Visit **www.halleonard.com/mylibrary** and enter the access code.

4

# Agony
from *Into the Woods*

Words and Music by
Stephen Sondheim

6

# Anyone Can Whistle

from *Anyone Can Whistle*

Words and Music by
Stephen Sondheim

**Slow and gentle**

*fermata second time only

# Children Will Listen

from *Into the Woods*

Words and Music by
Stephen Sondheim

# The Ballad of Sweeney Todd

from *Sweeney Todd*

Words and Music by
Stephen Sondheim

65

70

77

82

87

92

98

104

110

115

122

# Johanna
### from *Sweeney Todd*

Words and Music by
Stephen Sondheim

# Pretty Women

from *Sweeney Todd*

Words and Music by
Stephen Sondheim

**Languid but steady, non rubato (♩ = 72)**

# Night Waltz

from *A Little Night Music*

Words and Music by
Stephen Sondheim

75

81

88

95
(V)

102

109

116

123

129

136
2

144

(opt.)

# Not While I'm Around

from *Sweeney Todd*

Words and Music by
Stephen Sondheim

**Più mosso, sempre rubato**

**Tempo primo**

# Send in the Clowns

from *A Little Night Music*

Words and Music by
Stephen Sondheim

# Sunday

from *Sunday in the Park with George*

Words and Music by
Stephen Sondheim

# With So Little to Be Sure Of

from *Anyone Can Whistle*

Words and Music by
Stephen Sondheim

# You Must Meet My Wife

from *A Little Night Music*

Words and Music by
Stephen Sondheim

# Not While I'm Around

from *Sweeney Todd*

Words and Music by
Stephen Sondheim

**Più mosso, sempre rubato**

# Pretty Women

from *Sweeney Todd*

Words and Music by
Stephen Sondheim

# Send in the Clowns

from *A Little Night Music*

Words and Music by
Stephen Sondheim

# Sunday

from *Sunday in the Park with George*

Words and Music by
Stephen Sondheim

# With So Little to Be Sure Of

from *Anyone Can Whistle*

Words and Music by
Stephen Sondheim

# You Must Meet My Wife

from *A Little Night Music*

Words and Music by
Stephen Sondheim

**Più mosso**